LONDON TRANSPORT BUSES, TRAMS AND TROLLEYBUSES IN PRESERVATION

MALCOLM BATTEN

AMBERLEY

First published 2023

Amberley Publishing
The Hill, Stroud
Gloucestershire, GL5 4EP

www.amberley-books.com

Copyright © Malcolm Batten, 2023

The right of Malcolm Batten to be identified
as the Author of this work has been asserted in
accordance with the Copyrights, Designs and
Patents Act 1988.

ISBN 978 1 3981 1877 5 (print)
ISBN 978 1 3981 1878 2 (ebook)

British Library Cataloguing in Publication Data.
A catalogue record for this book is available from
the British Library.

Typesetting by SJmagic DESIGN SERVICES, India.
Printed in the UK.

Introduction

Ninety years ago, in 1933 London's buses, trams, trolleybuses and Underground network were placed under a common ownership when the London Passenger Transport Board was formed, trading as London Transport. The world's largest municipal transport organisation, it served an area that stretched over 25 miles each way from Charing Cross, the heart of London. The Central Area, roughly corresponding to the Greater London area, had red buses. Beyond this the Country Area had green buses, and Green Line express services linked London with towns on the fringes of the Country Area.

Bus operation in London dated back to 1829 when George Shillibeer first brought horse buses to London, and the Underground was the world's first underground railway system, with the original section of the Metropolitan Railway opening in 1863. Recognition of this heritage had already begun under one of London Transport's chief antecedents – the London General Omnibus Company. They had retained one of the famous B type buses of the First World War period along with its successors and had celebrated the centenary of omnibuses in 1929 by constructing a replica of Shillibeer's horse bus. London Transport continued this tradition by retaining other historic items, including the last remaining Beyer Peacock 4-4-0T locomotive that worked on the Metropolitan Railway before electrification, which had survived by being used on the remote Brill branch until this closed in 1935. However, while a growing collection of artefacts was being put aside, there was no museum to display them.

This situation changed in 1961 when the first part of the Museum of British Transport opened in the former Clapham bus (originally tram) garage on 29 March 1961. It was divided into six galleries, featuring models, paintings, maps, tickets, uniforms and other miscellanea. One gallery was entitled 'London on wheels'. In the rear yard, some of the pre-war buses saved by London Transport, of K, S and NS types were displayed at the time.

The main hall opened on 29 May 1963 with 35,000 square feet available for large exhibits. As well as railway exhibits, the new hall also housed the collection of buses, trolleybuses and trams that London Transport had by now amassed. There were the horse buses. Motor buses included the B type B 340 of 1911, 1920 K type K 424, 1923 S type S 742, 1931 AEC Regent ST 821, and 1930 AEC Regal T 219 in Green Line livery. There was the first production trolleybus for London, the 'Diddler' No. 1. Built in 1931 for London United, who were absorbed into London Transport in 1933, this had been retained in working order and was run in service on the last day of London trolleybuses, 8 May 1962.

London's trams had ended ten years earlier in 1952. An example of the London County Council E1 type, 1908-built No. 1025 was saved and restored to 1948 condition. Trams such as this would have operated out of Clapham during its days as a tram depot. There was also a former County Borough of West Ham tram and a former London 'Feltham' tram in the colours of its subsequent owner Leeds Corporation.

The Museum of British Transport closed in 1973 as the rail exhibits were removed to the new National Railway Museum at York. A replacement museum known as the London Transport Collection opened at Syon Park in 1973. The single-storey hall housed all the London exhibits from Clapham, and seven other vehicles for which space had been previously unavailable. Although successful, the Syon Park site lacked further expansion space. More crucially, it was considered too remote from the passing tourist trade. Therefore, London Transport remained on the lookout for other alternative premises in a more central location.

The solution to London Transport's problem came when the Covent Garden market moved to the site of the former BR steam depot at Nine Elms in 1974. The Covent Garden site became a conservation area. The old Flower Market, which is listed Grade II, was converted in 1978–79 to become the new London Transport Museum. The new museum was opened by Princess Anne on 28 March 1980. Ideally suited in the heart of a tourist area in Central London, this has been the home of the London Transport Museum ever since. A makeover in 1993 saw the insertion of a mezzanine floor to increase the exhibition space available. A further refit between 2005 and 2007 has enabled the museum to take on the wider role of the various aspects of public transport under the Transport for London remit. The Covent Garden site is supplemented by the Museum Depot at Acton, which holds the reserve collection. This opened in October 1999 and is publicly open on selected weekends and for pre-booked tours.

The London Transport Museum buses could also sometimes be seen at events such as the HCVC London to Brighton Historic Commercial Vehicle Run, first held in 1962.

Private preservation of London buses started in 1956 when AEC Regal T31 was bought by a group of six people including Ken Blacker, Michael Dryhurst and Prince Marshall for the sum of £45, to become the first privately preserved bus. Many others followed and the London Bus Preservation Group was founded by eleven preservationists in 1966. They drew up a set of six aims including 'To bring together for their mutual benefit all known owners of ex-London Transport vehicles where the object of ownership is the preservation of the vehicle for historical purposes'. At this stage there was no mention of acquiring premises to house vehicles or of creating a museum. However, the building that became the Cobham Bus Museum in Redhill Road was acquired by the London Bus Preservation Trust (as it had then become) in 1972. The LBPT collection would grow, and the cramped Cobham premises became unfit for purpose. Eventually, in 2011, the magnificent new London Bus Museum opened at Brooklands, near Weybridge.

Many hundreds of ex-London buses are now in private preservation. Some are with individual owners, others with groups and a number have been retained by modern-day bus companies such as Arriva as part of a heritage fleet. Major collections are those of the London Bus Company/London Vintage Bus Hire, Ensignbus and TimeBus. As well as being used commercially for wedding hires, advertising and film work, etc., many of these vehicles can frequently be seen at bus rallies, garage open days and running days where they can once again perform the work they were built for, carrying passengers over routes that may themselves have passed into history.

London Transport's Country Area buses and Green Line coaches were hived off to the National Bus Company on 1 January 1970 to form a new company: London Country Bus Services. The Routemaster buses would later be sold back to London Transport for further service.

The LPTB (London Transport) had designed buses specifically for its own requirements, to be built by AEC or Leyland, and up to the 1930s had also bodied many vehicles themselves. After the Routemasters and AEC Merlins they switched to mainly 'off-the shelf' designs including Daimler Fleetlines and Leyland Nationals in the 1970s.

London Transport itself ceased to exist in 1984. From 29 June 1984 London Regional Transport took over London Transport from the GLC. Then from 1 April 1985 a new wholly owned subsidiary, London Buses Ltd, took on the operation of buses. In April 1989 London Buses was split into eleven regional operating units, plus London Coaches, who ran the sightseeing operation. This was in preparation for eventual privatisation in 1994–95. From 3 July 2000 a new Mayor of London was appointed, who took over responsibility for London Bus Services Ltd and a new regulatory authority called Transport for London (TfL). Some of the vehicles bought by the privatised companies have themselves now passed into preservation. For space limitations these have not been included in this book.

A number of Routemaster buses can still be found working on sightseeing tours in London. There are those used by Brigit's Afternoon Tea Bus Tours and by London Necrobus on their Ghost Bus tours. A new company, Londoner Buses, started a tourist route A with Routemasters from Waterloo station to Piccadilly Circus on 15 October 2022. Others are owned by companies specialising in wedding hires, film work, corporate catering, etc. However, as all these are operated commercially rather than as sidelines to preservation they have been excluded from this selection.

This book traces the development of London Transport bus, tram and trolleybus preservation and shows some of the vast variety of vehicles that have survived, both on static display and operating.

All photos are by the author except where credited.

Museum Collections

Museum of British Transport
Clapham High Street, London, SW4

Large Exhibits Section Opening 29 May 1963

Come ! See them at Clapham

Buses of yesteryear · Vintage road-vehicles
Historic locomotives · Railway coaches and wagons
Royal train suites

OPEN
10 am to 5.30 pm on weekdays

ADMISSION
Adults 2/6 Children 1/6 Special arrangements for School Parties

HOW TO GET THERE
UNDERGROUND : Northern Line to Clapham Common
BUSES : 35, 37, 45, 88, 118, 137, 155, 181, 189, to Clapham Common Station
GREEN LINE : 711, 712, 713
BRITISH RAILWAYS : Clapham, Clapham Junction or
Balham & Upper Tooting, then by bus

VISIT ALSO
The Railway Museum, York — exhibited are some of the
earliest locomotives in existence.
The Great Western Railway Museum, Swindon — here is
the thrilling story of the Great Western Railway.

The
London Transport
Collection

Syon Park
Brentford
Middlesex

Pride of place among the London buses on display in the main hall at the Museum of British Transport when it opened in May 1963 was the ex-London General B340, which had been preserved by the London General Omnibus Company. B340 was a 1911 AEC B type with LGOC O18/16RO body, representing the first really successful mass-produced London buses. First introduced in 1910, 2,678 were built in the next three years, including single-deck versions. Over one thousand were pressed into military service during the First World War. (Reg Batten)

Some of the other London buses on display in the main hall. On the left is S742, a 1923 AEC S type with LGOC O28/26RO body, while on the right is ST821 of 1931, an AEC Regent. The scale of progress made during the 1920s is evident with the ST now sporting a roof, enclosed staircase, a windscreen and pneumatic tyres. (Reg Batten)

B43 was also preserved by the Auxilliary Omnibus Companies Association in memory of the role these vehicles (including B43) played during the First World War transporting troops in France and Belgium. This bus had also been inspected by King George V at Buckingham Palace in February 1920. Nicknamed 'Ole Bill', it appeared regularly in parades until it was retired to the Imperial War Museum in 1970. It is seen here as it was displayed in 2005 after the layout there had been amended. More recently it was exhibited at the London Transport Museum as part of their celebrations of the centenary of the First World War. It is now displayed at the Imperial War Museum's No. 5 Hanger at Duxford.

After Clapham closed in 1973 the London Transport exhibits moved to a new location at Syon Park known as the London Transport Collection. Space was rather restricted within Syon Park, making photography somewhat difficult. Here we have T219, the 1931 AEC Regal with Duple body, in Green Line livery. This had previously been at Clapham and before that had been entered in the inaugural 1962 HCVC London–Brighton Run. Behind it is TF77 (FJJ 774), which had not been previously exhibited at Clapham. Photographed in 1977.

Syon Park had been home to the London Transport Museum since 1973 but the site was cramped, lacked expansion space and was too remote from the main tourist traffic. Syon Park closed at the end of 1978 to allow the exhibits to be moved to the new location at Covent Garden once the site was prepared. To mark the closure, a Final Gala Day and Collector's Sale was held on Sunday 17 September 1978. On display at this occasion was trolleybus 260 from the London Trolleybus Preservation Society, which had originally been intended to be preserved by LT but was rejected and then privately purchased.

A view inside the new London Transport Museum at Covent Garden in May 1980 with AEC Q type Q55 and an RF behind. On the left is 'Diddler' trolleybus No. 1 with its central single headlight, a vehicle preserved by London Transport in the continuing tradition set by the LGOC in the 1920s.

Above left: Seen in 1984 is tram 290, originally West Ham 102, which at this time carried London Transport livery.

Above right: The first Routemaster, RM1, has been retained as part of the London Transport Museum collection. Here it is posed outside Covent Garden on 20 June 2010 to mark thirty years since the opening there.

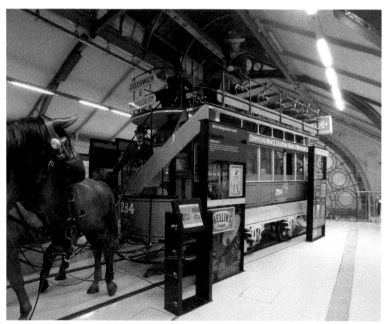

London Tramways Company horse tram No. 284 was built by John Stephenson & Co. of New York in 1882. This is housed on the mezzanine floor at Covent Garden.

The visiting B43 and former West Ham tram 102, now back in West Ham livery, are on display in 2014.

Routemaster RM1737, RT 48925 (the last built), and Leyland Cub C94 are on display in 2014.

The London Transport Museum is backed up by the London Transport Museum Depot at Acton, which houses the overflow vehicles, Underground trains and much of the archive material. This is only open to the public on a limited number of weekends each year. Seen here in 2014 are ex-Metropolitan 'Feltham' tram 355 and the unique rear-engine Routemaster FRM1.

On the same day in 2014 are Q1 trolleybus 1768 and RM2, in the process of being restored to its original style front end and green livery (see also p. 32).

The London Bus Preservation Group acquired premises at Redhill Road, Cobham, in 1972, which became the Cobham Bus Museum. A first public 'open day' came in April 1974, and from this grew the annual Cobham Gathering. The yard behind the building usually housed a themed display and in April 2003 this congregation of 1920s buses was staged. From left to right are K424, K502, S742, Chocolate Express Leyland LB5 No. B6, and Dennis D142. K424 and S742 are from the London Transport Museum, D142 from the LBPT and the others privately owned.

Outside the museum site in 1977, passengers wait to board GS34, which was bought by an LBPG member in 1976. This was donated to the museum in 1999. It was later housed off-site for many years but reappeared in 2019 with the display of rarities and unrestored buses held there in June. In 2021, the display hall at the London Bus Museum was reorganised and GS34 became one of the exhibits on display.

Seen in April 2003, this is AEC Regal T357 (GN 8242). New to Queen Line in 1931, it was taken over by London Transport and rebodied by Weymann in 1935. In 1943, this and a few others were fitted with producer gas trailers, painted camouflage grey and used on route 462 to the Vickers Aircraft Works at Weybridge (of which the Cobham museum premises was a former part). In 1945 it had been exported by the War Department for use in Germany and later sold off for use in France. Discovered stored in France, it was repatriated in March 2003.

The new London Bus Museum opened at Brooklands in 2011. Seen inside are this pair of double-deck horse buses representing the garden seat type on the left and earlier knifeboard style with longitudinal bench seat on the right.

The internal layout was revised in 2021 following closure for Covid. Seen here are side-engined AEC Q type Q83, currently in Green Line livery, and rear-engined Leyland Cub CR16, representing innovations in chassis design of the 1930s. CR16 was rescued from Cyprus, to where it had been exported in 1979 and emerged fully restored in 2007.

Seen inside in 2012 is NS174. The remains of this were acquired in 2004 and work is being undertaken to build a replica open-top body (the London Transport Museum example has a covered top and is on pneumatic tyres). On the right RLH53 was undergoing restoration (since completed).

The June 2019 'rarities' display saw the LT Museum's restored 'scooter' 1931 AEC Renown LT1076 posed alongside the LBPT's as yet unrestored LT1059, which was recovered from Teignmouth, Devon, in 2003.

For the 23 October 2022 TransportFest at the London Bus Museum, the 1925 Dennis D142 was presented newly repainted in its original colours of the London Public Omnibus Company. Here it is being backed into position ready for the official presentation.

Tram and Trolleybus Preservation Sites

The Crich Tramway Village in Derbyshire has the largest collection of trams in the UK, with examples from many parts of the world. This is former London County Council (LCC) 106, which dates from 1903. This was taken in 1983.

At Crich in 2015 is London Transport 1622, built in 1912. This is the only working example of the LPTB E/1 type, of which over 1,000 were built. It was reconstructed from the original lower deck, found in Hampshire after use as a shed. The remains of a separate upper deck provided parts and patterns for making a replacement and the body is mounted on 'Feltham' bogies. The restored tram entered service in 1997.

Also seen on the same day in 2015 is former Metropolitan Electric Tramways Company experimental tram 331 of 1929 – a predecessor to the later 'Felthams'. This was sold to Sunderland Corporation in 1937. It was sold early by LT as being non-standard. The central entrance prevented it being fitted with a plough for operation on the LCC conduit system.

The East Anglia Transport Museum at Carlton Colville near Lowestoft has resident London HR/2 tram 1858 of 1930. This museum was founded in 1965 when a group of local enthusiasts who had bought the body of Lowestoft tram No. 14 in 1962 decided to develop a museum in which to run it. The land was donated by Mr Bird, the founder and first chairman of the society. An early link was forged with the London Trolleybus Preservation Society, owners of London No. 260 at Reading. As a result, the museum installed wiring for both trams and trolleybuses to run around the site.

The East Anglia Transport Museum is the only place where both London trams and trolleybuses operate together. Seen here visiting is London Transport trolleybus No. 1. Built in 1931 for London United, it is an AEC 663T with UCC H32/24R bodywork. On withdrawal it was retained by London Transport for preservation and was operated on the last day of London trolleybuses in 1962. Now it remains part of the London Transport Museum collection. (Geoff Silcock)

Seen in 2015 are trolleybuses 260 and 1521, both owned by the London Trolleybus Preservation Society. No. 260 had been chosen by LT to be preserved as a representative London trolleybus. Ken Blacker as advisor from the HCVC considered that trolleybus 260 was not the most suitable as it had been fitted with a post-war staircase. K2 class No. 1253 was chosen instead along with Q1 class No. 1768 to represent the final class of trolleybuses. No. 260 was then destined for scrapping but two members of the Reading Transport Society, Tony Belton and Fred Ivey, heard about this and intervened to purchase the trolleybus for £125.

The largest collection of trolleybuses in Britain can be found at the Sandtoft Transport Centre near Doncaster. Awaiting their turn for restoration in 1987 are two London Transport vehicles with 1201 on the right.

Move forward to 2016 and this is trolleybus 1348, a 1939 Leyland. This is on long-term loan to Sandtoft from the Transport Museum Society of Ireland.

Another place that has trolleybus wiring installed is the Black Country Museum at Dudley. Normally resident trolleybuses from the West Midlands are used but London Transport 1521 visited in June 2006. This was the last London trolleybus to operate in service, and the first to run under wires in preservation, at Carlton Colville in 1971.

Significant Anniversary Events

Easter parade.

Horse bus service.

In 1979 London Transport celebrated 150 years since George Shillibeer first introduced the omnibus to London in 1829. There were a series of events in which the vehicles saved by London Transport and its predecessor, the London General Omnibus Company, would be paraded, alongside those preserved privately by the LBPT and other organisations and private individuals. The first major event of the year was a rally and parade in Battersea Park on Easter Sunday 15 April. Some forty vehicles, including the replica Shillibeer horse bus, took part in the parade. This knifeboard horse bus is being followed by one of twelve Routemasters repainted in Shillibeer style livery.

Also at Battersea Park, it was fitting that the prototype RT1 should be on show, just a week after the last RTs had ended service on route 62 from Barking garage. This vehicle was nearly lost to UK preservation. It had remained with LT until 1978 when sold into preservation but was then exported to the USA. It was repatriated in the 1980s and later given a full restoration at a cost of over £200,000. Despite an offer from abroad it was finally acquired by the London Bus Museum in 2010, who had to raise the asking price of £150,000 within a year through an appeal fund.

The main event of the year was on Sunday 8 July, almost 150 years to the day since George Shillibeer had started his pioneer horse bus service. Several vehicles including the 1929-built replica of Shillibeer's horse bus ran over part of the original route from London Wall to Paddington before joining the main rally in Hyde Park, where it was seen. 1979 was probably the first time the horse bus had run on the road since the 1929 centenary celebrations. It had most recently been an exhibit at the now closed London Bus Collection at Syon Park.

Also at Hyde Park was CR14, a 1939 Leyland Cub with a rear-mounted engine, the first such design for London, and with a LBTB B20F body. This was part of the LT Museum collection at the time but has since been sold into private preservation. Although these mostly worked in the Country Area, some were used as rush hour extras on Central Area routes and this was in the Central Area red livery at the time.

Between 9 July and 30 September, passengers had the opportunity to ride on a horse bus from Baker Street and around the inside perimeter road of Regent's Park to London Zoo. Three horse buses were used and this, a *c*. 1885 Andrews Star Omnibus Co. garden seat bus new to London General.

On Sunday 6 August 1989, the RT/RF Register and London Transport Museum organised 'RT50' to celebrate fifty years of the RT type entering service. Vehicles ran between Moorgate Finsbury Square where RT1677 and RT4421 are seen to Covent Garden. RT1677 was the last to be delivered from Park Royal bodybuilders with cream upper-deck window surrounds.

Above: The first and last. RT1 and RT4825 were posed outside the London Transport Museum in Covent Garden as part of the RT50 celebrations.

Right: RM 50 Anniversary.

**50ᵗʰ Anniversary of the Routemaster
Finsbury Park - 24ᵗʰ & 25ᵗʰ July 2004**

The RM 50 Anniversary held in Finsbury Park in July 2004 was organised by the Routemaster Operators and Owners Association to mark fifty years since the first Routemaster. London Transport Museum's RM1 is seen ahead of the numerical last Routemaster RML2760. This at the time was part of the Stagecoach heritage fleet but was passed on to the London Bus Preservation Trust on loan in 2013. Some Routemasters were still in front line service at this time. The last would not be withdrawn from route 159 until December 2005.

RM3 was acquired by LBPG in 1974, the first Routemaster to be preserved. It was rebuilt to its 1957 condition and regained the original number RML3 (having a Leyland engine) in time for RM50, where it is seen.

Eighty years of Green Line was celebrated on 17 July 2010 with a Road Run over the original route from Embankment to Guildford. Thirty vehicles, ancient and modern, participated and here Green Line-liveried RT3232 leads former London Country RP90 at Barnes. RT3232 is owned by Ensignbus.

On arrival at Guildford the vehicles parked up at the Arriva garage where there was a part open day. Three generations of T type AEC Regals are seen here. On the right is the LT Museum's T219 of 1931 with Duple bodywork; in the middle is T504 of 1938 with LPTB bodywork; and on the left 1948 T792, a Country Area bus with Mann Egerton bodywork.

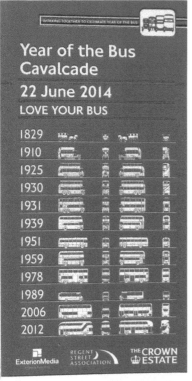

Above: The origins of the Associated Equipment Company (AEC) lay when Arthur Salisbury Jones of the London Motor Omnibus Company began to build his own buses for the company. Few were built before a merger with the London General Omnibus Company in 1907. A standard bus incorporating best practice was designed – the X type, which was superseded by the B type. In 1912 the Underground Group, who now owned the LGOC, set up AEC Ltd as a separate commercial company. The centenary was celebrated in 2012 by a road run through Walthamstow where the factory was originally based before moving to larger premises at Southall in 1927. Vehicles then gathered at the Pumphouse Museum. Two classic AEC designs – and RT and RF – take part in the run.

Left: Year of the Bus Cavalcade, 2014.

2014 was designated by Transport for London as 'The Year of the Bus' with a number of special events and open days. The main event on 22 June was a cavalcade of London buses spanning their history from the South Bank to Regent Street, which was closed off for the day and where the vehicles then parked up on display. Leading the cavalcade from the South Bank was the oldest surviving motor bus that ran in London. This is LN 7270, a 1908 Leyland X2, originally London Central 14. This was restored by Mike Sutcliffe. who has since transferred it to the London Transport Museum, along with the Chocolate Express Leyland LB5 (see p. 13).

This was followed by newly restored B2737 of the London Transport Museum, built in 1914. This was seen on the South Bank arriving to take up position in the cavalcade.

C4 had recently been restored by owners Ensignbus. A Country Area Leyland Cub of 1935, it has a Short Bros B20F body. These vehicles were replaced by the GS class in the early 1950s.

Single-deck S type S433 of 1922 on display at Regent Street, where the sheer number of people made photography challenging. This is part of the collection of Barry Weatherhead, Woburn Sands. Note that this has both a windscreen and pneumatic tyres fitted.

Also at Regent Street is Tilling No. 935, a 1922 Tilling-Stevens TS3A with replica body. This was one of the vehicles from the late Michael Banfield's collection, which was auctioned at Bonham's and raised world auction price records for double-deck buses. This sold for £216,540, while former 1922 London General S454 sold for £281,500. Both buses were subsequently placed on loan to the London Bus Museum at Brooklands by their new owner.

Trolleybus 1768 from the LT Museum collection was towed into position and displayed at Regent Street. As trolleybus wiring was never extended to the West End, this was probably the first time a trolleybus had ever appeared in Regent Street.

Ten years on from RM50, RM60 was also staged in Finsbury Park. This impressive line-up of the type has RM2217 on the left. This was the highest numbered standard RM and the last to work in daily bus service in December 2005. It was retained by then owners Arriva as part of their heritage fleet, as shown on the advertising panel. In 2022 Arriva announced the end of their heritage fleet: 'It is with great sadness that Arriva London announces that our Heritage Fleet operation will cease at the end of 2022 and the vehicles will be available for sale for further use or preservation'.

After many years out of the limelight, the London Transport Museum returned RM2 to its original radiator style and green livery in time to feature at RM60.

With the centenary of the First World War in 2014, B2737 was repainted in wartime livery and with boarded-up windows to recreate the way these buses were used to carry troops to the front during the war. It made several appearances at remembrance events including travelling to France. Here it takes part in the 2014 Lord Mayor's Show. A 'New Routemaster' in British Legion poppy vinyls is seen behind.

Garage and Works Open Days

An open day was held at Aldenham Works on 25 September 1983 before its closure in 1986. On hand was Cobham Bus Museum's RF332, which had been converted as a recovery/towing vehicle.

An open day at Chiswick Works on 11 August 1985. Among the vehicles on display were the LT Museum's ST821, once a resident at Clapham and later Syon Park. Now it had been repainted in Country Area green. Alongside is privately preserved post-war STL2692 of 1946. This had seen later service with Grimsby-Cleethorpes before being saved.

An open day at the London Country South West's Addlestone garage on 9 April 1989, the day of the Cobham Gathering, sees three RLH vehicles posed there. Green RLH's were based here until 1971 for routes 436 and 463, which encountered a low bridge.

Left: An open day at Holloway garage on 3 July 1993 and among the vehicles present are STL469 and LT165, both from the London Transport Museum collection

Below: An open day at Fulwell garage on 24 July 1994. Among the vehicles present was RFW14, one of a batch of short AEC Regal IVs with ECW bodies intended for coach tours and private hire work.

Not a garage open day as such, but the closure of the old Kingston bus station on 22 October 1995 was marked by a display of vehicles that used to operate out of the adjacent garage, which had closed in 1984. It had later reopened in 1987 as a minibus base for Stanwell Buses (Westlink). Kingston was particularly noted for the number of RF routes and was the location for the last of these in LT service in 1979.

An open day held at Leyton garage on 10 May 1997. Emerging to work a trip for the visitors is the LT Museum's RT4712.

In August 2006, in a surprise move, Stagecoach sold their London bus operation to Australian investment group MacQuarie Bank for £263.6 million cash. The new owners traded as the East London Bus Company. The two East London Bus Company garages in Waterden Road, Stratford, were scheduled for closure as they came within the area that would be redeveloped as the Olympic Games site. A farewell open day was held at Waterden Road on 16 February 2008 at which RML 2760 and T1, both part of the heritage fleet, are seen together. In October 2010 Stagecoach announced that they had bought the business back for a cut-price £52.8 million.

Stockwell garage has staged a number of open days. One was held in 2014 as part of The Year of the Bus celebrations. Among the vehicles present were NS1995 from the London Transport Museum and privately preserved RT1702. The NS class had been introduced in 1923 with solid tyres, no windscreen and open top. Later on, as technology improved and legislation was relaxed, pneumatic tyres, windscreens and covered tops were fitted to members of the class and NS1995 represents the final form of the type. Contrast this with NS174 (p. 15).

Also on display in 2014 was V3, the one-off Volvo Ailsa which had recently been restored by owners the London Bus Company to its original dual-door format. Opened in 1952 as part of the tram replacement programme, when it was built Stockwell garage had the largest unsupported concrete roof span in Europe, and its architectural importance is recognised with a Grade II listing.

Fifty buses (including fifteen Routemasters) were given gold paint or vinyl livery to mark the Queen's Golden Jubilee in 2002. Also painted gold was London Transport Museum's RT4712. Along with Arriva RM6, by then part of the heritage fleet, it was on display at the Ash Grove garage open day in April 2017. When first painted in 2002 the RT had a white band and Transport for London fleetname. The band changed to purple in 2003 to mark the fiftieth anniversary of the coronation.

Garage open days are often accompanied by trips over sections of local routes, past or present, by some of the buses present. On the occasion of a Potters Bar garage charity open day in July 2018, RML2272 is seen at Cockfosters station having arrived on a section of route 298. A modern vehicle on the same route is behind.

The MD class Scania Metropolitans were associated with Plumstead garage in the latter part of their life. The sole surviving example in the UK, MD60, now part of the Ensignbus heritage fleet, was giving local rides at the open day held on 30 October 2021 to mark forty years of the garage.

Heritage Fleet Vehicles on Bus Routes

Some operating companies have staged one-off events with their heritage vehicles perhaps to raise money for charity. This could be for special event days such as Red Nose Day or Children in Need. Alternatively, it might be to mark the takeover of a route or the ending of tenure on a route.

A small bus rally was held in the car park behind Barking Town Hall in April 1987, and for the occasion Ensignbus ran their preserved RT3062, which at that time was in yellow and silver livery, over their recently acquired route 62, which had been the last route to be worked by RTs until 1979. The bus was photographed in Becontree on 5 April 1987. Note the LRT contract roundel sticker. They also put out RT3232, which was in the fleet livery of blue and silver at the time. It has since been repainted in Green Line colours (see p. 27). This was also repeated in 1988.

Stagecoach lost the contract for trunk route 25 in June 1999, which passed to First Capital on retendering. For the last week of Stagecoach operation, Blue Triangle's semi-preserved RT3871 was hired for all-day service. It is seen at Mile End on 25 June.

Stagecoach-owned RMC1461 was restored to original appearance and Green Line livery in 1994. Although painted primarily for display purposes, it still saw use on the 15, as here at Paddington on 23 August 1995. When the route eventually lost its Routemasters on 29 August 2003, RMC1461 was donated to Cobham Bus Museum.

Timebus, St Albans, are another company that have built up a large heritage fleet of ex-London buses. In the 1990s they also had some tendered routes for Hertfordshire CC around Watford, on which they often put out their heritage vehicles. RM1571 was at Watford Junction station on 27 September 1995. Note the full use of the LT blind boxes.

In August 2003 Stagecoach painted RML 2456 into its original London Transport green livery for the last day of Routemasters on route 15. It then was put to work on surviving RML route 8 (despite the requirement for buses on London tendered routes to be painted red). On 30–31 May 2004 it and RML 2760 were run over a series of current and former routes served by the company. Here it is in Wanstead blinded for the former route 10 to Abridge.

Routemaster Routes Last Days Guest Vehicles

During the final rundown of Routemasters on central London bus routes, the last day was often accompanied by guest heritage or preserved vehicles running over the route – sometimes vehicle types that had operated on the route in the past. These could be either carrying fare-paying passengers or just invited guests. When route 8 ended on 4 June 2004 one notable 'first' was London Transport Museum's RM1 performing on stage service for the first time in nearly thirty-five years!

On the last day of route 19 on 1 April 2005, as well as Routemaster types, there were three RTs from Ensignbus, RT3871 from Blue Triangle, and privately owned RT1702. This is Ensignbus RT1431 near Finsbury Park. This is one of a batch, RT1402–1521, that had bodies built by Craven Ltd that were non-standard, noticeably by having an extra window on each side. Being non-standard, they were sold off early.

Also on 1 April 2005, the LBPT ran their STL2377 over route 19 all the way to Tooting Bec for invited guests only. Here it is seen opposite Sadlers Wells theatre. The Arriva Routemaster behind was on route 38, which would retain the type until 28 October 2005.

When it was the turn for the 38 to finish with Routemasters on 28 October, the LBPT put out ST922, which shadowed part of the route, although not carrying passengers. Here it lays over at Green Park.

Some unusual guest vehicles did carry fare-paying passengers on the last day of RMs on the 38. One of these was Ensignbus's RLH61, seen with a very full load crossing Cambridge Circus, Holborn.

Perhaps one of the most unusual of the guest vehicles was this 1949 former Hants & Dorset Bristol K6A, also at the time owned by Ensignbus. This was captured turning into Piccadilly from Hyde Park Corner. It carried a London Transport badge on the radiator, in the style in which this, and other such vehicles, were hired by London Transport when new to cover a vehicle shortage.

However, the most unusual vehicle on the 38 was RMF1254, the unique front-entrance Routemaster. Remarkably, this was the first time it had ever worked on London stage service, having only been used as a demonstrator, then on the BEA contract, before being sold to Northern General. Now preserved and restored by Imperial Buses, it was hired by Ensignbus for one round-trip on the day.

The last Routemaster-worked route was Arriva's 159 Marble Arch–Streatham, which finally succumbed on 9 December 2005. A total of twenty-four guest vehicles ran including RTs, an RTW and Routemasters. The service Routemasters were due to end by 13.30. The honour of being the last to depart fell to RM2217, seen here in Whitehall. The open-top bus was for media photographers and there was a police escort. It finally reached Brixton garage at 14.07.

Heritage Bus Operated Routes

From 8 April to 27 October 1972 London Transport hired a preserved bus to work a scheduled route. Former Tilling and later General 1930 AEC Regent ST922 was hired from Obsolete Fleet. It ran daily on a circular route 100 from Horse Guards Avenue and was sponsored by Johnnie Walker whisky, whose adverts it carried. The bus had been bought for preservation by Prince Marshall in 1966 and stored until 1971, when it was renovated by LPC Coachworks Ltd. ST922 was hired again in 1973, although the routing was altered. It also ran each summer until at least 1977, in which year the route 100 ran between Trafalgar Square and the Tower of London. Each year it ran it was sponsored by different companies whose products it advertised.

In 1988–89 Essex County Council funded a Sunday leisure bus service 622 every two hours from Harlow to Great Yeldham, taking in a number of tourist attraction villages such as Dunmow, plus Castle Hedingham and the Colne Valley Railway. Blue Triangle had the contract that specified vintage vehicles, and normally used ex-London Transport RTs. Weymann-bodied RT2799 was taken on 7 August 1988 at Harlow bus station.

A new innovation for 1990 (and repeated in 1991) was Essex County Council Summer Sunday (and bank holiday Mondays) 'heritage' leisure route 612, which ran all the way from Romford to Colchester in some three and a half hours. On its (indirect) way it passed the East Anglian Railway Museum at Chappell and the Colne Valley Railway at Castle Hedingham. It was run by Blue Triangle, who usually put out former London Transport RF401. The bus is seen leaving Romford on 17 June. The passengers are probably mainly transport enthusiasts.

In 1993 Metrobus operated Wealdsman 746, a Sunday and bank holiday service from Bromley to Tunbridge Wells between 29 May and 25 September, running every two hours. Former London Transport RF255 was used along with a Dennis Dart. The RF is seen here attending a bus rally in April before the start of the service.

In 1990 London & Country had operated 'Guildford Leisure Routes' 706–9 from 22 July to 2 September with hired former Green Line RF136. In 1992 they bought former London Transport GS13, which had been operated in 1991 by Sussex Bus on a Chichester tour for a new Surrey Hills Leisure Service 433 to Dorking via Clandon House and Polesden Lacey. This ran three journeys on Sundays and bank holidays. This is seen at Guildford in 1994.

London & Country's operation of vintage buses on Sunday leisure services was expanded in 1993 to include RT3775 on the 473, which linked East Grinstead station where the bus is seen in 1994 to the Bluebell Railway, which at that time terminated at Kingscote station, where there were no car parking facilities. This ran until 1998 when the RT was sold and a Dennis Dart from Metrobus took over the service.

Although Routemasters ceased being used in normal service in 2005, they continued to be used on two 'heritage' routes launched in November 2005. Stagecoach worked the 15, which paralleled the normal service between Tower Hill and Trafalgar Square daily from around 9.30 to 17.30. RM 324 was seen at St Paul's Cathedral on 22 September 2008. Note the traditional London Transport livery and dedicated publicity for the London Transport Museum.

For HM the Queen's Silver Jubilee in 1977, twenty-five Routemasters were repainted in silver, and renumbered as SRM 1–25. Firstbus repainted RM1650 as SRM3 in 2004, the identity it carried in 1977 (although with different adverts then). After the withdrawal of Routemasters from normal service this was retained and used on heritage route 9, where it is seen in the Strand on 9 June 2006. The other RMs used were repainted in London Transport livery.

On 20 July 2013 Ensignbus RT8 is seen turning out of Park Lane at Marble Arch while working the Wartime London Tour. This bus, built in 1939, is painted in wartime style livery with the white mudguard edges to aid visibility in the blackouts. It re-entered service in 2010 following restoration. In 2013 this tour ran from 2 April to 31 October on Tuesdays, Thursdays and Saturdays.

The Epping Ongar Railway reopened as a steam and diesel heritage railway in May 2012. As trains are not able to work into Epping station where both platforms are used by LUL, on operating days, bus route 339 provides a link from Epping station to the railway at North Weald, with some journeys continuing to Ongar and (since 2014) Shenfield. The service is registered as a route so that local passengers can be carried as well. Former London Transport vehicles from the associated London Bus Company fleet are used. The route number 339 is that of the original Country Area route, which ran from Warley, south of Brentwood, to Harlow via Ongar and Epping. RTL1076 was at Epping station on 30 June 2013.

Former London Transport Green Line AEC Routemaster RCL2260 pauses at Ongar in 2018 with an afternoon service to Shenfield station. These buses originally ran on Green Line routes 721 from London to Brentwood and 722 from London to Corbets Tey, Upminster.

Bus Rallies

Bus rallies have greatly developed since the 1970s, and while some events have come and gone, others have become a regular part of the annual calendar. Vehicles from the London Transport Museum and London Bus Preservation Group have been regular attendees at some of the more established events. Certain rallies also include opportunities for visitors to ride on some of the vehicles, either around the site where the rally is held (at Detling for example) or on former routes in the local area.

The London Transport Museum have been regular supporters of the HCVC (now HCVS) London–Brighton Run since it began in 1962. London General K424 (XC 8059) took part in the 1962 run and again for the fiftieth run in 2011 where it is arriving at Brighton. This dates from 1921. The type was first introduced in 1919 as the successors to the B type and was the first to have the driving position alongside the engine rather than behind, thus making better use of the available space. Withdrawn in 1932, it was put aside for preservation by London General and passed to London Transport. After participation in the 1962 run, this became an exhibit at the Museum of British Transport at Clapham from 1963 to 1973.

At Brighton in 1974 but 'just visiting' were not one but two ex-London Transport TDs. TD89, a 1949 Leyland PS1 with Mann Egerton bodywork, is seen, and behind it is the more familiar TD95 (JXC 288) from the London Bus Preservation Trust at Cobham. This was probably attending as a tender vehicle for Dennis D142 (XX 9591), which was a Run entrant. TD89 was later acquired by Timebus, St Albans, and fully restored in 2021 (see p. 83).

Making its first Brighton appearance in 1977 was T31, a 1929 AEC Regal with LGOC body. This is a particularly significant vehicle as it was the last ex-LGOC bus to work for London Transport and the first London bus to be privately preserved. Bought in 1956 for £45, by now this was owned by Norman Anscombe and had been rebuilt from front entrance to its original rear entrance style since 1974 and also refitted from diesel to petrol engine. Today this forms part of the London Bus Preservation Trust collection.

STL2692 at Showbus, Uxbridge, in June 1975. This batch of 1946 AEC Regent II STLs (STL2682–2701) for the Country Area had Weymann H30/26R bodies. STL2692 was sold to Grimsby Corporation in 1955 and on withdrawal by Grimsby – Cleethorpes in 1968 was bought by for preservation, being entered on the 1968 London–Brighton Run.

1977 saw the repatriation of London Q1 trolleybus 1812 from Santandar – Astillero in Spain. Destined for the British Trolleybus Society at Sandtoft and eventual rebuild to London condition, it was exhibited at Uxbridge in 'as acquired' condition with offside entrances, etc. Alongside is TXV 909, a former London AEC Mercury tower wagon, 1076Q, by now with Reading Transport. This had towed the trolleybus to the rally.

London Transport never had any of their eighty-four-strong GS class in Central Area red livery. However, this did not deter the owners of preserved GS67 from creating a fascinating 'might-have been' by painting it in red and entering it at the 1979 Showbus Rally.

In 1960 London Transport purchased three AEC Reliance buses, RW1–3, with dual-door Willowbrook bodies for experimental one-man-operation in the Country Area. After three years these were all sold to Chesterfield Corporation. RW2 and RW3 both later passed into preservation and RW2 is seen at the former Weybridge aircraft factory while on the bus link to the Cobham Bus Museum for the 1980 Cobham Gathering.

The 18 July 1982 London Bus Rally was held at the premises of Ensignbus at Purfleet. On display was Q69, which had been rescued after many years of open storage in a yard at Goodmayes. The body of this was later scrapped and the chassis acquired by the LBPT for spares.

Prototype Leyland-engined Routemaster RML3 (later RM3) became the first privately preserved Routemaster when it was acquired by the LBPG in 1974. This shows how it looked in April 1990. All the four prototypes had received standard production style radiator grilles in later life with London Transport, but this has since been rebuilt to the earlier style (see p. 26).

At a rally in Redhill during August 1993 is LT165, the 1931 AEC Renown with LGOC body from the London Transport Museum. This was displaying wartime white mudguard markings and blast netting over the side windows. Alongside is the LBPT's much-travelled AEC Regent ST922 of 1930.

After deregulation in 1985, London bus routes were put out to tender. London Buses, as successors to London Transport, set up some 'low-cost' units to compete for tenders. One such was Orpington Buses, who trading as Roundabout won the tenders for routes around Orpington in 1986 with minibuses such as this Volkswagen LT55 with Optare City Pacer bodywork – the first of their type to enter service. These were replaced by new Iveco buses in 1993 and OV2 was then preserved by the London Transport Museum. It is seen here at the Netley Rally.

In 1973 London Transport bought six Metro-Scania buses for comparison trials on route S2 against the newly introduced Leyland National to determine a successor to the unsuccessful AEC Merlins and Swifts. The Leyland National found favour and the Metro-Scanias were sold to Newport Corporation Transport in 1978. MS4 was later preserved by a group in Newport. On 1 January 1998 it was taking part in the Friends of King Alfred running day at Winchester. King Alfred Motor Services, Winchester, had bought three Metro-Scanias themselves before selling out to the National Bus Company in 1973.

The Leyland National became a standard type for London Transport in the 1970s. LS98 is one of a number that have been preserved and was at East Grinstead in 1999.

Many preserved London buses have been repatriated after being exported following withdrawal. Now with Ensignbus, RTW335 was shown at Wisley Airfield in 2004 in 'as acquired' condition.

From 1978, London Transport opted for two standard double-deck designs – the Leyland Titan developed from the B15 prototype and the MCW Metrobus. The first of each type has passed into preservation – Titan T1 with London Vintage Bus Hire and Metrobus M1 with Ensignbus. They are seen together at Wisley Airfield in 2005.

In 1973 London Transport introduced four new routes serving some previously unserved roads using Ford Transit minibuses. When passenger loadings outgrew these minibuses on routes B1, C11 and W9 they were replaced in 1975/6 by seventeen Bristol LHS buses with standard ECW bodywork. These were the only LT buses with manual gearboxes. BS5 is preserved and was entered on the 2005 HCVS London–Brighton Run.

The London Bus companies were privatised in 1994–95. Some of the vehicles taken over have been preserved in their post-privatisation liveries. RMLs 2731 and 2620 both carried the attractive style adopted by Metroline and are seen together at the 2009 North Weald Rally.

We saw the non-standard livery used by low-cost unit Roundabout earlier (see p. 56). Another low-cost unit was Bexleybus at Bexleyheath, who adopted a blue/cream livery similar to that of Eastbourne. This livery later fell foul of new regulations in 1990 that all LRT companies should be red, and Bexleybus itself lost most routes on retendering in 1990. T888 is preserved in Bexleybus colours as a reminder of this brief interlude. Wisley Airfield, 2010.

London's Fleetlines proved unpopular and were sold off early, many having a longer lifespan with subsequent owners. Three preserved examples are seen here at North Weald in 2010. Nearest is DMS2357, one of the final B20 type with modified engine compartment to reduce noise.

A most unusual sight at Dunsfold Aerodrome, site of the 2011 Cobham Gathering, was RT4779 displayed as a body frame while undergoing a thorough restoration. This was subsequently completed and the bus has been repainted in Country green livery.

S454 was the other bus from the former Michael Banfield collection that was acquired by Mr Maybury along with the Tilling-Stevens (see p. 30). After appearing at Regent Street, it was later entered in the 2014 Alton rally before being placed on loan to the London Bus Museum at Brooklands.

The Bus Reshaping Plan of 1966 called for a move to single-deck one-person-operated buses with flat fares. London Transport ordered the 36-foot AEC Merlins and later 33-foot AEC Swifts in both dual-door and single-door versions. They proved unreliable with high maintenance costs and were withdrawn after a short lifespan. Many Merlins were later exported including to Malta. Nevertheless, some have survived into preservation and on the Epping Ongar Railway at North Weald in 2018 this gathering of seven of the type was achieved. The middle one, SM88, was in the colours of subsequent owners AI, Ardrossan, at the time.

The theme of the Epping Ongar Railway bus rally in February 2019 was Green Line. Two visiting vehicles on display at North Weald were T499 from Ensignbus and TF77 from the London Transport Museum. The TF type was the first for London with an underfloor engine. After the prototype and TF2–13, which were private hire coaches, TF14–88 were Green Line vehicles.

At the Epping Ongar Railway bus rally held on 8 September 2019 the London Bus Company's RF136 appeared specially repainted in this 'one-off' livery. This had been applied to a modified RF by London Transport as a back-up to the RC class in these colours on Green Line route 705 but was not approved and never ran as such in public.

After buying Titans and Metrobuses, London Transport purchased small batches of the Leyland Olympian, Dennis Dominator, MCW Metrobus 2, and Volvo Ailsa for comparison trials before deciding on the Olympian. A total of 260 L class Leyland Olympians with ECW bodywork were then ordered in 1985 for delivery in 1986–87. L97 was at the South East Bus Rally at Detling Showground in 2022.

Making a welcome return to the rally scene after an absence for several years was Inter-Station Cub C111, which was entered in the 2022 HCVS London–Brighton Run. Eight of these vehicles were built in 1936 with Park Royal bodies for a service linking the London main stations at night when the Underground was closed. They had extensive luggage space below the raised rear portion and carried this unusual blue/cream livery.

B1609 has been preserved by Barry Weatherhead for many years and made a fine sight when it made a rare appearance at the final Showbus Rally at Redbourn in September 2022.

Not all rally entrants are in pristine condition! Both these vehicles have been fully restored in the past but when seen at Showbus, Redbourn, in 2022 RTW497 on the left was in course of a repaint while RTL1348 had recently changed ownership after being stored out of use for many years and was in course of restoration again. The RTL was one that saw service in Jersey after withdrawal by London Transport.

Classic buses at a classic location. Members of the Routemaster Owners Association have an annual get-together at the famous Ace Café at Stonebridge Park off the North Circular Road. Here four buses are posed together in December 2022. RM2116, second left, is preserved in the livery it was given in 1983 to celebrate fifty years of London Transport.

Running Days

A more recent feature, mainly since the 1990s where preserved vehicles carry passengers over routes. No fares are charged, but enthusiasts can purchase a timetable that raises funds for the participants. The events are organised by societies including the London Bus Museum. Vehicles may come from the LBPG, London Transport Museum collection, the heritage fleets of Ensignbus, London Vintage Bus Hire, Arriva, etc., and private owners. The event may be to mark a significant anniversary in the history of a route. Former types that ran that route may feature. Long-lost variations and extensions to the route may also feature. Alternatively, the buses may cover a group of routes in a particular area, perhaps to mark the anniversary of a particular garage. With the introduction of the ULEZ low emissions zone, while the historic vehicles are allowed to operate, the more modern preserved buses of the 1980s/1990s have been restricted to the area outside the zone, which in 2022 was set at the North Circular and South Circular roads.

Country Area Running Days are usually centred on a particular town rather than a specific route. Although mainly featuring the green Country Area buses and Green Line coaches, red Central Area buses often participate, and indeed in LT days it was quite common for vehicles to be loaned between the areas. With the longer routes, especially the Green Line routes, normally only a part of the route will be operated. However, there may be 'feeder' services to and from the event, intended to bring and return vehicles from their base, which will carry passengers over other routes or sections thereof.

The Ensignbus running day, normally held on the first Saturday in December, is slightly different. Although the operating area of Ensignbus around Grays and Tilbury and based on Thurrock Lakeside is within the former LT Country Area, they do not attempt to recreate former Country routes. Instead, they have created a pattern of special routes based around their area with extensions to nearby towns and heritage attractions. Also, unlike the other events, a rover day ticket is sold, which is also valid on regular Ensignbus services. As the Ensignbus heritage fleet contains many ex-London vehicles these will regularly feature alongside their other vehicles and various guest vehicles.

While this book confines itself to running days within the former LT Central and Country Areas, there are such events held throughout the country, and former LT vehicles may participate in any of these. One event that predominantly features former LT vehicles, especially Routemasters, is the annual running day from Warminster to Imber, the 'lost' village on Salisbury Plain that was requisitioned by the Army in preparation for the Normandy invasion.

RFs from Dalston garage worked route 236 from Leytonstone to Finsbury Park via Hackney and Dalston. RF486 is seen with a backdrop of the Arsenal Tavern on a recreation held on 1 April 2005.

A first running day at Slough and Windsor was staged by The Amersham & District Motor Bus Society on Sunday 17 April 2005. This was an ambitious affair with twenty routes being run in full or in part. A highlight was the running of route 442 to Burnham Beeches for the first time since the route was axed in 1958. RF366 is seen on arrival. On this occasion it was fitted with a non-standard front panel.

Bus routes to Chingford used to terminate at the impressive Royal Forest Hotel until 1968, but since then have terminated at the station. The North London Transport Society organised some running days whereby buses once again departed from the hotel and this was the scene on 11 September 2005.

RF366 sets off from Slough on route 335 to Gerrards Cross. The crews will often dress in period uniforms and issue tickets with the traditional Gibson ticket machines. This Central Area RF is one of those built without a front entrance door, intended for crew operation.

A running day based on Hertford, Hitchin & Stevenage was organised by Country Bus Rallies on 4 June 2006. RF4 sets out from Hertford for Tewin. This was one of the original batch of twenty-five built for private hire work, which were only 27 feet 6 inches long as opposed to 30 feet for all the rest. Somewhat surprisingly, seven of this batch survive.

The Hemel Hempstead running day of 25 June 2006, and red RF406 has arrived at the village of Chipperfield on former route 319.

A variety of vehicle types lay over at Hemel Hempstead bus station on 25 June 2006.

A running day based around the Croydon and Sutton area on 15 April 2007 sees RT190 at Wallington. This carries the early post-war livery style with cream around the upper-deck windows. It also has the restricted blind display from this time of shortages.

A running day based on Loughton held on 9 September 2007 sees former RF operated routes 20A and 254 being recreated at the station, while a green RML works as a duplicate on former Green Line route 718.

A pair of RTs at Loughton. RT624 in front was the last in passenger service with London Transport when the class was finally withdrawn from route 62 at Barking on 7 April 1979. It is now preserved by Ensignbus.

It's back to the 1930s as STL441 gets an outing at a Slough running day on 11 May 2008. This 1934 AEC Regent has a body built by the London Passenger Transport Board at Chiswick and forms part of the London Bus Preservation Trust collection. It was at the old Brunel bus station in Slough, now demolished and replaced (see p. 85).

Vehicles lay over in the now closed bus station at Hemel Hempstead on 22 June 2008. In the foreground is RT1499, the second of the pair of Craven-bodied RTs in the Ensignbus heritage collection.

When the RF class was due for replacement, London Transport originally intended to use the AEC Merlin MB class or AEC Swift SM class. But the licensing authorities indicated that on certain routes 7 feet 6 inch wide vehicles should be used and LT chose the Bristol LH with ECW bodywork. Ninety-five of the BL class were delivered from 1975, the last three being purchased by Hillingdon Borough Council for council-sponsored route 128. BL49 is at Hemel Hempstead on 22 June 2008. This bus was originally registered OJD 49R. Although the BLs were all red buses, London Country also bought Bristol LH buses.

It is 22 June 2008 and RF667 has arrived at the village of Sarratt while partaking in a running day from Hemel Hempstead. The driver adjusts the blinds for the return journey.

The village green at Sarratt boasted this fine bus shelter.

There were a couple of running days based on Gravesend in the 2000s that featured preserved vehicles from both London Transport and Maidstone & District, who also served the town. Here in July 2008 green RF633 threads through part of the town centre, which has gated access restricting it to pedestrians and buses. Note the NF (Northfleet) garage plate and running number plate fitted for the day – just one of the lengths to which the owners go to achieve realism on these occasions.

On 22 March 2009 a running day was held to mark thirty years since the end of RFs. Up to twenty-seven RFs were booked to attend. The buses assembled and laid over at Sandown Park racecourse. In this view at least twenty-two of the type can be seen, in a variety of livery styles.

Also in passenger use that day was TD95, seen taking on a full load in Kingston for a trip to Walton-on-Thames. This forms part of the London Bus Preservation Trust collection.

On a running day from Hertford, RF633 makes a photo stop for passengers in the village of Widford while working over former route 350 to Much Hadham on 6 June 2010. Until November 1964 Widford had a railway station on the former branch line to Buntingford.

At the Red RF Group Colindale running day on 29 August 2010, Timebus, St Albans, RF491 is seen at Highwood Hill, Mill Hill, on a short working of route 251. It carries the Timebus fleetname and grey lining around the windows.

A running day over route 38 on 17 June 2012 sees RTL139 from the LBPT running through Dalston against a backdrop of typical terraced housing. The satellite dish is a later addition!

Taking part in a Hemel Hempstead running day on 19 August 2012, GS13 has arrived at Chesham.

The Amersham running day has been one of the longest established Country Area events. On 7 October 2012 T792 heads out on a local route. This batch of AEC Regals T769–98 were the last half-cab single-deckers bought by London Transport and were delivered for the Country Area in 1948. They had B31F bodies by Mann Egerton with a sliding door. This is in the only survivor.

A running day at East Grinstead in 2013 and GS2 heads out of town against a background that had probably not changed much from when the class was in regular service there.

The classic London Transport livery as many people will think of it – cream band and gold underlined fleetname. RM5 has been restored to this form as part of the Arriva heritage fleet. Here it is seen on a running day to commemorate 100 years of route 76 on 20 July 2013. Many of the Routemasters on heritage route 15, which was still running at this time, also carried this livery style, as can be seen on the Stagecoach RM travelling the opposite way at St Paul's Cathedral.

A running day based on Watford Junction station on 30 March 2014 gave opportunities for running over both Central and Country Area routes. STL2377 display blinds for route 142 while behind can be seen one of the vehicles that at the time operated the route. This was run by Arriva from the former Country Area garage at Garston (since closed).

At the Watford running day on 30 March 2014, GS13 sets off from the station. No blinds are set but in the blind box is a label that reads 'On hire to Knightwood Coaches'. Knightwood Coaches introduced a route in September 1963 from Watford to Elstree Aerodrome (Hog Lane) that ran just three journeys a day on Tuesdays, Fridays, Saturdays and Sundays. By 1972 the Sunday service had gone and only one journey a day ran. The company was acquired by Campbell Consultants in 1975 who in turn passed to Mullaneys Coaches in 1984. Knightwood once owned GS75, so the recreation by GS13 was appropriate.

RML2440 sets off on a journey to Napsbury Hospital – a reminder of the days when routes ran to provide access for visitors to mental hospitals that were located in the country – out of sight and out of mind? Napsbury, near London Colney, was opened in 1905 and closed in 1998, now redeveloped for housing.

A running day on route 11 on 2 November 2014 saw RT1 carrying passengers through central London. Here it precedes an RTL on a journey in Whitehall.

The eight XF class Daimler Fleetlines spent most of their life at East Grinstead, passing on to London Country in 1970. Unlike the XA class of Atlanteans, these did not get sold to Hong Kong and two (XF1, XF3) have survived. Here XF3 returns to its old stamping ground at the 2015 East Grinstead running day.

The London Transport Museum maintain the unique rear-engine Routemaster FRM1 in running order and it sometimes operates at running days. Here it is seen at East Grinstead in 2015. The Routemaster had failed to find sales outside London other than to Northern General. With AEC becoming part of British Leyland, who already had the Leyland Atlantean, Daimler Fleetline and Bristol VR rear-engine models, the FRM was seen as having no commercial future and was dropped with London Transport opting for the Fleetline as their double-deck choice in the 1970s.

On 25 November 2018, a running day was held over former routes 104 Barnet – Moorgate and 104A Barnet-Golders Green. The 104 was the route on which the first batch of RMLs – RML880–903 were employed when new in 1961. Several of the batch survive and here RML899 leads two others at Moorgate Finsbury Square while the back of another can just be seen having departed. This was originally registered WLT 899 and is now with London Vintage Bus Hire.

A running day to mark forty years since the end of the RF class in April 1979 was held on 24 March 2019. This was centred on their final operating area between Kingston, Weybridge and Staines. Other later types also participated, and this is Country Area SM90 at Staines bus station. The SM class were still being delivered at the time London Country was split off in 1970, although SM90 dates from 1968.

On 30 March 2019, forty years since the final withdrawal of the RT class from route 62 at Barking in April 1979 was celebrated. There was an open day at Barking garage and vehicles running over local routes. The once familiar sight of a line-up of the type in the garage yard was recreated. Seven of these buses including the nearest RT4548 and the others with roof-mounted marker lights are from a batch repatriated from Canada in 2010 by Roger Wright of London Vintage Bus Hire. They were used there for sightseeing tours on Prince Edward Island and retain the lettering from this period.

Organised by the LBPT, local routes were recreated, and in the afternoon the RTs ran in convoy to the town centre and back. Roofbox-fitted RT1784 is in the lead in this view, with blinds from the final RT route.

A running day at High Wycombe was organised on 1 September 2019 by the Amersham & District Motorbus Society to commemorate the centenary of the Amersham & District Motorbus & Haulage Company, which was absorbed by the LPTB in 1933. Vehicles ran over ten former local routes of the 1960s and RF600 is seen at Holmer Green on former route 364.

On 18 April 2021 the RLH class returned to their last red route, the 178 Maryland Station–Clapton Pond where they ended in 1971, or as close to it as modern road layouts permitted, given that part of the route around Stratford had been redeveloped for the Olympic Games in 2012. With Covid restrictions still in place, this was a photographic run only with no passengers carried. Of the nine examples of the class that survive in the UK, eight were running (the other being under overhaul). Green RLH48 leads red RLH23 at Old Ford.

There was a route run over route 93 Putney Heath–Epsom–Dorking on 9 October 2021 organised by the LBPT. In the afternoon roofbox-fitted RT1705 prepares to depart from Putney Heath with a trip to Epsom. The 'New Routemaster' behind is on route 37, a route which would be featured in October 2022.

On 7 November 2021 a
running day was organised
centred on Muswell Hill.
With excellent weather all
day, here at the Broadway
RF401 of London Vintage
Bus Hire is setting off
on another trip down to
Finsbury Park on route 212.
This route has now become
the W7.

Highlight of the day was
a couple of journeys on
route 212 by TD89, recently
restored by owners Timebus,
St Albans. I caught this at
Crouch End heading south to
Finsbury Park.

RM613, owned by
RM613 Owners Ltd, has
been restored to original
1960 appearance complete
with rear wheel covers, brake
cooling grilles and period
advertisements. This is seen
on former route 134A later
on the same day in Colney
Hatch Lane.

Left: Route 101 running day.

Below: The first LBPT route running day of 2022 was on the 26 March in glorious sunshine. The featured route was the 101 North Woolwich–Wanstead, once LT's most frequent route. Highlight of the day was the operation of 1946 Guy Arab II G351. This vehicle had been allocated to Upton Park garage and worked on the 101 back in the 1940s. The shops in the background here at East Ham High Street North would all have been there back then, though with different tenants. The arch was added in 1992.

RTs were the mainstay of the 101 for many years and fifteen examples featured on the day. RT1798 arrives at North Woolwich and passes the disused Grade II listed 1854 station building, at one time a railway museum. RT1798 is owned by the Claude Jessett Trust, Hadlow Down near Uckfield.

On 13 June 2022 the second of the year's route running days featured route 81 Hounslow–Slough and its variations. RT4779 departs Slough for Hounslow. The futuristically designed Slough bus station, opened in 2011, contrasts with the classic lines of the RT bodywork.

In 2022 ninety years of Victoria coach station was celebrated with a series of events. On 24 July historic coaches ran trips between Victoria and Hammersmith. There were also heritage buses on route 11 from the coach station to Aldwych. RT1705, nicely presented with period advertisements, passes along Buckingham Palace Road.

Also recreated on the day was a portion of former Airbus service A1 from Victoria to Heathrow. This ran from Victoria to Hammersmith via Hyde Park Corner. The first MCW Metrobus M1 stands at the open-air portion of Hammersmith bus station. This is now with Ensignbus, Purfleet hence the LT-style PT (Purfleet) garage code.

A running day based on Hendon was held on Sunday 20 November 2022 to mark thirty-five years since closure of Hendon (AE) bus garage. Vehicles operated over five routes – the 13, 32, 140, 183 and N59. RT4275 lays over at the Brent Green terminus of route 140 to Queensbury. The blinds are showing a short working to Mill Hill Broadway.

DM1052 heads along the North Circular Road on its way to take up duties on route 183 as part of the Hendon running day. Some of the proceeds from programme sales for this event were donated to the BBC Children in Need appeal.

The final London Fleetline, DM2646, was painted in this 'Shillibeer' livery, sponsored by British Leyland for the 1979 London Transport fifty years celebrations. Now preserved by Ensignbus, it is seen at Thurrock Lakeside during the 2021 running day. It is setting out on route X55, which will take it to Gravesend via the Queen Elizabeth II bridge over the Thames.

The first Dennis Darts in London entered service in 1990 and had bodies by Carlyle Works. DT39 worked for the Roundabout fleet of Selkent at Orpington where they replaced minibuses such as OV2 (see p. 56). This was taking part in the 2021 Ensignbus running day and was taken at Upminster station.

T499 was repatriated from Australia and is preserved by Ensignbus. After restoration, it made a first appearance at the 2013 running day painted in the style in which many of these vehicles operated during the Second World War when Green Line services were suspended and they were converted as ambulances for the American Red Cross. It was then repainted in Green Line livery for the Year of the Bus parade in 2014.

Commercial Work

RT1702 was one of four that inaugurated the Circular Tour of London in 1951, during the Festival of Britain. It later passed into preservation. In 1976 it was displayed outside the Victoria & Albert Museum, who were holding a twenty-five-year commemorative exhibition on the Festival of Britain. RT 1702 was to feature again in 2000, as an exhibit in the Millennium Dome exhibition.

In July 1990 a 'Garden Festival' was held at Gateshead. This was one of a number of such events in the 1980s/90s, others including Liverpool and Glasgow. At Gateshead an internal tramway was installed for visitors and a selection of preserved trams were brought in to operate on it. These included former Metropolitan tram 331 from Crich (see p. 18), which had later been sold to Sunderland. It was sponsored by British Steel and painted in this promotional livery.

In 1992 former Green Line RMC1462 was owned by Nostalgiabus and painted in Green Line colours. That year the Model Railway Club's annual exhibition was held here at the Royal Horticultural Hall, Westminster, and the bus had been hired to operate a shuttle service to and from Victoria station. Also in use were RF492, then owned by North Mymms Coaches, and RLH23, both in red livery. Note the LT pattern blind display.

From time to time, preserved buses are featured in period films and on one occasion in November 1992 I encountered STL441 from the London Bus Preservation Trust so employed at the Bank of England in the company of a contemporary car and taxi.

In 2022 London Vintage Bus Hire painted RML902 in this white livery specifically for wedding hire work. It was taken passing through Victoria amid contrasting architectural styles on 27 May.

Preserved Service Vehicles

As well as buses, some of the many service vehicles that served London Transport have also passed into preservation. For this section, I have limited the selection to former buses, but there are also a range of other vehicles from vans to heavy recovery trucks.

London Transport 971J is the only surviving front-entrance STL and this was due to its conversion for tree pruning in 1953. Built in 1936 with Weymann bodywork for the Country Area, these buses had a central staircase but no doors. In service they were cold in winter and suffered from windswept litter being scooped into the body. The STL was replaced by a purpose-built Ford Thames Trader lorry registered 969 ELR in 1963. 971J was pictured at Kingscote station on the Bluebell Railway.

One of a batch of breakdown tenders that were converted in 1950 from 1933 AEC Regent buses of the STL class with new Chalmers of Redhill van bodies. Four of these vehicles remained in use until at least 1970 and all four have since passed into preservation. Besides 830J, AXM 649 (ex-STL43) seen here they are JJ 4379 (ex-STL162), which became 832J, AGX 520 (ex-STL169), which became 738J and AGX 517 (ex-STL175), which became 739J.

London Country substantially rebuilt former LT RLH44 to become a uniform issue vehicle, numbered 581J. It was later preserved, and its unusual appearance can be appreciated here in this view at the 1987 Southsea Rally.

RM1368 had its upper deck destroyed in an arson attack in 1973. Rather than rebodying it, London Transport apprentices at Aldenham works converted it to a single-deck vehicle with rear doors used by the experimental department at Chiswick. Sold into preservation in 1990, it is seen in 2000.

The 'Supercar' was created in 1991 for a TV campaign jointly funded by Network SouthEast and London Transport to promote one-day travelcards. Former DMS1515 was rebuilt to create this bus/tube car/NSE class 321 promotional unit. As well as appearing in the commercial, it also visited the Lord Mayor's Show and Bus of Yesteryear Rally. Now preserved by the London Bus Company, it was seen here at the North Weald Rally in 2012 promoting the Epping Ongar Railway, which had just reopened that year as a heritage line.

Ex-London Transport Vehicles in Subsequent Owners' Liveries

Many London Transport buses (and also trams and trolleybuses) were sold on for further work with other owners and some of these have been preserved in the liveries of their subsequent owners.

When the Country Area was hived off to form London Country Bus Services, they initially retained the LT green livery but with a yellow band and their fleetname and 'flying polo' logo. The Routemasters would later be sold back to London Transport as LCBS adopted one-person operation. RML2412 carries the initial LCBS livery style but with the grey hub caps of National Bus Company style. Taken at a Hemel Hempstead running day on 22 June 2008.

From 1973 LCBS adopted the standard National green livery. Only two RTs lasted long enough to receive this and both later passed into preservation, where they have retained this livery. RT604 is seen posed at the entrance to Pinewood Studios during a running day based in Slough. 11 May 2008.

Several of the GS class Guys were sold off early when their routes were withdrawn as uneconomic. GS40 passed to West Bromwich, where it gained their elaborate and attractive livery. Now preserved locally, it is seen at West Bromwich in 1987.

Former RTW178 saw subsequent service with Stevensons of Uttoxeter and has been preserved in their livery. Note that the blindbox display has been modified while with Stevensons. It is seen at the Showbus Rally at Duxford Airfield in 2006 along with a number of London RF types.

After deregulation in 1986, many companies throughout Great Britain bought former London Routemasters either as a way of competing against existing companies or as a way of fighting off potential competition. Among the purchasers of Routemasters was Reading Mainline, who competed against Reading Transport. Former RMs 1859 and 1990 retain their livery and are seen together at the 2019 Alton rally. Note the full use of the front blind displays.

Some vehicles have been preserved in subsequent owners' liveries because they were substantially rebuilt or rebodied by these owners. RT2494 was one of four RTs that went to Guernsey between 1987 and 1994 where they were rebuilt as open-toppers. After withdrawal it returned to the mainland for preservation and is seen here at Brooklands in 2014.

London Transport's wartime 'utility' buses were all sold off in the early 1950s. Daimler CWA6 D27 passed to Southend Corporation, who had the original body replaced by a new Massey lowbridge body in 1954. In this form it would not be authentic for the bus to be in LT livery and GLX 913 is now part of the Ensignbus heritage fleet in its Southend colours. It is seen at Thurrock Lakeside taking part in the 2021 Ensignbus running day.

Acknowledgements, Bibliography and Further Reading

Baker, Michael H. C., *London Transport Since 1933* (Shepperton: Ian Allen, 2000)

Christie, David, *The London to Brighton Commercial Vehicles Run 1968 to 1987* (Stroud: Amberley Publishing, 2018)

Jenkinson, Keith A., *Saved for Posterity: Bus and Coach Preservation* (Stroud: Amberley Publishing, 2018)

Simmons, Jack, *Transport Museums of Western Europe* (Newton Abbot: David & Charles, 1971)

Slater, D. J., *Preserved Buses, Trolleys & Trams* (2nd edition) (Birmingham: D. J. Slater, 1993)

Smith, Graham, *London Buses A Living Heritage: Fifty Years of the London Bus Museum* (Kettering: Silver Link, 2017)

Wharmby, Matthew, and Rixon, Geoff, *Routemaster Requiem* (Hersham: Ian Allan, 2006)

Preserved Buses (2021 edition) (London: The PSV Circle, 2021) and earlier editions

Buses (bi-monthly/monthly magazine) (Hampton Court, Ian Allan, 1949 onwards, now Key Publishing)

Bus & Coach Preservation (monthly magazine) (Portsmouth: Presbus Publishing, 1998 onwards, now Meteor Books)

Various publications, including fleet lists and newsletters by the London Omnibus Traction Society. This is the principal society for enthusiasts of London Transport and its successors, and anyone with an interest in the London bus scene past and present is recommended to join. www.lots.org.uk